I0429208

TABLE OF CONTENTS

ACRONYMS

COIN	Counterinsurgency
JP	Joint Publication
MOP	Measures of Performance
MOE	Measures of Effectiveness
FM	Field Manual
LLO	Logical Line of Operation
MACV	Military Advisory Command Vietnam
VC	Viet Cong
MNF-I	Multi-National Forces Iraq

ILLUSTRATIONS

TABLES

INTRODUCTION

In the twelve years of the war on terror, Iraq and Afghanistan have dominated military

conversation. Both wars, arguably, began in a conventional manner. The term conventional

assumes the definition of state-sponsored, uniformed forces engaging other state-sponsored forces

with conspicuous use of firepower and maneuver. While news organizations provided a constant

update on each war, the average viewer could easily discern progress of the offensive. In

Afghanistan, coalition forces, including the local Northern Alliance captured Mazar-i-Sharif to

the jubilant celebration of its inhabitants allowing the establishment of an airbase in the heart of

the enemy's country. Coalition Forces then captured other major population hubs such as

Kandahar, Jalalabad, and the capital city of Kabul. The Taliban forces were obviously routed.[1]

Reports of the surrender of Iraqi forces, the videos of the liberated population dancing in the

streets and the vivid image of the toppling of a statue of Saddam Hussein demonstrated to the

world audience that the coalition forces were winning the war.[2] No planner could have imagined

a more effective means of routing the enemy in both cases. The evidence of success was

everywhere. Within a few months of both invasions, coalition forces toppled the former regime

and the future of both Afghanistan's and Iraq's government laid at the mercy of foreign powers.

Then something changed. In both countries, fighting resumed. This time, however, the fighting

was not conducted by state-sponsored elements carrying out orders and employing a combination

of fire and maneuver. Instead, the coalition forces faced an insurgency. Now military practitioners

---

[1] Center for Military History Publication 70-83-1, *The United States Army in Afghanistan: Operation Enduring Freedom October 2001-March 2002*, 13-15.

[2] "Saddame Statue Topples with Regime", BBC.co.uk, April 9, 2003, under On this Day, http://news.bbc.co.uk/onthisday/hi/dates/stories/april/9/newsid_3502000/3502633.stm (accessed on February 28, 2013).

could not measure progress in terms of enemy destroyed or captured, cities controlled or statues toppled.[3] A new war had begun and required a new plan for prosecution.

How does the military commander know if he or she is winning in counterinsurgency? The answer is not as obvious in COIN as it is in conventional war. It is, however, necessary to assess if one's actions are having the desired effect, but what should a COIN force measure? US Military Doctrine provides some guidance on establishing metrics.

Army Doctrinal Publication (ADP) 5-0, *Planning*, outlines the considerations an organization must make while planning for any mission. One consideration, the development of assessments, includes generating measures of performance (MOPs) and measures of effectiveness (MOEs). MOPs are used to determine if an organization is meeting the minimum standards for the accomplishment of assigned tasks. Specifically, if an organization, as part of an operation, is supposed to establish road blocks, train local security forces, and destroy an element of enemy forces, then that same organization can measure if they have accomplished these tasks. They can first measure how many roadblocks they establish, how many local security force personnel they train, and how many enemy platforms they destroy in a given engagement. They can even further determine if they have executed the roadblocks to a prescribed standard, if the training of the local security forces has enabled the security forces to perform certain tasks, or what type of enemy forces they destroyed. All of these determine if an organization is correctly executing tasks.[4] Next, and possibly more important, an organization must determine if these tasks contributing to mission success.

_____

[3] James Clancy and Chuck Crossett, "Measuring Effectiveness in Irregular War", *Parameters*, Summer, 2007, 90.

[4] Army Doctrinal Reference Publication 5-0, *The Operations Process* (Washington DC: Government Printing Office, September 2011), 5-2.

Ideally, each of these tasks would support an overall mission. For instance, road blocks and security force development could relate to a stability or defense mission while destroying enemy forces within an assigned area could relate to an offensive operation or area defense. In any operation, however, a commander and his staff must determine what tactical tasks will accomplish the assigned mission. Once they assign these tactical tasks, it is important to know that subordinate elements are executing the tasks to standard. It is also important to know that these tasks translate into mission success, thus the need for MOEs.[5]

JP 5-0 states, "MOEs are based on observable or collectable indicators."[6] If this is the standard, then it is important that MOEs do not become so intangible as to be no better than a guess. Even the US Army's Field Manual (FM) 3-24, *Counterinsurgency,* states that MOEs should be measurable, discrete, relevant and responsive.[7] US doctrine does acknowledge that in counterinsurgency, metrics can be challenging, but no less important.[8] However, with the criteria above, metrics should be something that exist in the tangible world and genuinely relate to winning. After all, measurements reduce uncertainty so that a commander can make informed decisions about how to dedicate his or her resources and know when to ask for more.[9]

Identifying metrics for counterinsurgency is a pressing need for the US army. Because insurgency is more common than conventional war, it is reasonable to assume that the US

---

[5] Joint Publication 5-0, *The Operations Process* (Washington DC: Government Printing Office, September 2011), 5-1.

[6] Joint Publication 5-0, *The Operations Process*, D-3.

[7] Field Manual 3-24 *Counterinsurgency* (Washington DC: Government Printing Office, September 2006), 5-7.

[8] Joint Publication 5-0, *The Operations Process*, III-45.

[9] Douglass Hubbard, *How to Measure Anything: Finding the Value of "Intangibles" in Business,* (Hoboken, New Jersey: John Wiley & Sons, Inc, 2010), Kindle electronic edition, 6.

military must maintain the ability to conduct counterinsurgency in a variety of environments.[10] In the last decade, the US military has fought against an insurgency in two countries that are completely different in terms of culture, geography, infrastructure, and concepts of governance. Units will continue to conduct training that requires staffs to develop metrics to assess the relevance of tactical actions. It is not satisfactory to ignore this important step in mission planning and execution assessment during training and then expect it to occur in a combat zone. This situation demands the need for a universal approach to developing metrics that is relevant to any counterinsurgency.[11] Do any metrics exist that satisfy this demand? If any metrics do exist that are common to all counterinsurgencies, then the military should include them in doctrine, expect them in the training environment and use them in actual counterinsurgency operations.

A common misperception is that counterinsurgencies are all different.[12] However, since an army cannot be formed and ready for every contingency, it is reasonable to attempt to identify if there are any universal metrics in COIN.[13] If one views effectiveness as being in a position of advantage instead of on a path to a specific endstate, then it might be possible to look at counterinsurgency in more general terms. Metrics should be evidence that the counterinsurgent has regained asymmetric advantage by decreasing the insurgent's anonymity and its ability to rely on terrain or the population.

---

[10] Max Boot, *Invisible Armies: An Epic History of Guerrilla Warfare from Ancient Times to the Present* (New York: Liveright Publishing Corporation. 2013), xx.

[11] James Clancy and Chuck Crossett, "Measuring Effectiveness in Irregular War" *Parameters*, Summer, 2007, 90.

[12] Austin Long, *On Other War: Lessons from Five Decades of RAND Counterinsurgency Research* (Santa Monica, California: RAND Corporation, 2006), x.

[13] Clancy and Crossett, "Measuring Effectiveness in Irregular War", 90.

Clausewitz argued that every war is a contest to overcome the enemy's means or willingness to fight.[14] This provides two very broad categories by which to determine which side holds the advantage. To convert these tasks into metrics, it is important to establish that the COIN force can affect either willingness or means, and that the COIN force can measure this effect. Measuring the means to fight immediately lends itself to satisfying the observable, collectible, measurable, discrete criteria which doctrine establishes, but it does not necessarily mean it is possible. Measuring the wiliness to fight, at first glance, appears to remain more subjective and require informed judgment. Both possibilities are worth exploring to determine which provides the more relevant and realistically achievable metric. The purpose of this monograph is to determine if measuring the trend in insurgent tangible resources is the best metric for determining which side holds the advantage.

A Note on Winning versus Victory

In order to alleviate confusion, it is important to understand that this monograph does not use winning and victory interchangeably. Winning is a present tense condition that can change over time. Victory refers to the final condition of a conflict. At any time during a football game, one can determine who is winning unless the score is tied. The victor is only decided once the game is over. In counterinsurgency, there are no tied scores. One side is always winning while the other is losing.[15]

---

[14] Carl Von Clausewitz, *On War*, trans. And ed. Michael Howard and Peter Paret (Princeton University Press, 1984), Kindle edition,77

[15] G. L. Lamborn, *Arms of Little Value: The Challenge of Insurgency and Global Instability in the Twenty First Century*, (Havertown, Pennsylvania: Casemate Publishers, 2012), Kindle electronic edition, location 3391; Frank Zimmerman, "Why Insurgents Fail: Examining Post-World War II Failed Insurgencies Utilizing the Prerequisites of Successful Insurgencies as a Framework", (thesis, Naval Postgraduate School, March 2007), kindle electronic edition, location 363.

One may argue that in order to know who is winning a war, the commander must first know what constitutes victory.[16] Only then can he or she measure progress toward achieving this goal. This is not the case. The desired outcome of a war is dependent upon the political reasons for starting the war and may change as the war unfolds.[17] Instead, if one views winning as gaining or maintaining an asymmetric advantage over the enemy, then this can remain constant no matter the political condition. If a force has an asymmetric advantage over the enemy, then it has the ability to achieve the desired political condition. As soon as the enemy mitigates the advantage, he has threatened the achievement of the political condition. So, while victory requires achieving a specific condition, progress toward victory, or winning, requires being in an advantageous position to achieve victory.

In conventional war, both sides agree to what constitutes advantage. While there is no formal handshake or contract involved, the common understanding of advantage pertains to firepower, maneuver, protection, leadership, and resourcing. For instance, in a western conventional conflict, more tanks is an advantage over fewer tanks, faster execution has an advantage over slower execution, tactical prowess has an advantage over tactical incompetence, more resources are better than fewer resources. The victory tends to go to the side that has the greatest advantage.[18] Asymmetry develops when one side grossly outmatches the other in terms of advantage. This is the case in insurgency.[19]

---

[16] Russell W. Glenn and S. Jamie Gayton, *Intelligence Operations and Metrics in Iraq and Afghanistan* (Santa Monica, California: RAND Corporation, 2008), 52.

[17] Clausewitz, *On War*, 579.

[18] Linda Beckerman, "The Non-Linear Dynamics of War", Science Applications International Corporation ASSET Group, 1999, http://www.calresco.org/beckermn/nonlindy.htm (accessed on March 11, 2013), 2.

Typically, insurgents do not have tanks, cannot conduct a brigade size maneuver against an objective or drop bombs from the sky. It would, therefore, be foolish for an insurgent to fight against these advantages. If he did try, insurgencies would be characterized by a truck with a big gun tied to the top trying to face down tanks. The tank's advantage is so obvious that the image is almost comical. An insurgent also typically cannot penetrate the base perimeter of a conventional force using overwhelming firepower and maneuver. The insurgent simply does not have the adequate means to tactically defeat a conventional force. Instead, the insurgent identifies that which does provide him with advantage and uses that to battle the conventional force.[20] Since the conventional force has superior firepower, armor, mobility, and resources in the form of weaponry, basing and vehicles, the insurgent must mitigate this advantage. In essence, the insurgent seeks to regain symmetry by using another element to gain an advantage in firepower, armor and mobility.[21] This element is anonymity.[22]

It is anonymity that provides the insurgent with the ability to plan, resource, move, stage and conduct attacks against the conspicuous conventional force.[23] It is anonymity that allows the insurgent to place a devastating device next to a tank without ever being threatened by the tank. Anonymity allows the insurgent to penetrate a base's perimeter defense so he can detonate an explosive in a dining facility without being threatened by the base defense apparatus. It is also

---

[19] David Galula, *Counterinsurgency Warfare: Theory and Practice* (N.P. Fredrick A Praeger, 1966),Kindle electronic edition, location 172.

[20] Clancy and Crossett, "Measuring Effectiveness in Irregular War", 91.

[21] Galula, *Counterinsurgency Warfare: Theory and Practice*, Kindle location 180.

[22] Geoff Demarest, *Winning Insurgent War: Back to the Basics* (Ft. Leavenworth, Kansas: Foreign Military Studies Office, 2001) 2, 17.

[23] Demarest, *Winning Insurgent War: Back to the Basics,* 20-26.

anonymity that allows the insurgent to move throughout the battlefield without armor. It also allows an insurgent to cross a border, obtain supplies, and reenter a country unmolested.[24] Without this advantage, the insurgent is completely at the mercy of the conventional force. However, if the insurgent can remain invisible, the conventional force cannot employ the tools that provide it with advantage.[25]

Anonymity provides the symmetry that insurgents do not have in a conventional fight. Since history confirms that gaining an asymmetric advantage over the counterinsurgent is not necessary for the insurgent to achieve his desired political condition, the insurgent is winning the moment he achieves symmetry.[26] This is why there are no tied scores in COIN.

Anonymity is not automatically guaranteed to insurgents. Either the terrain and geography or the population enable the insurgent's ability to remain invisible to the COIN force.[27] If terrain is favorable to the insurgent, he can operate outside the presence of the conventional force and the population at large. If the geography is favorable, he can resupply in areas outside the governments influence, often with the help or a third party. During the insurgency in Moldova, counterinsurgents enjoyed the support of the population, while the insurgents enjoyed the support of Russia. The Moldovan government's forces were unable to deny the favorable geography to the insurgent, and were eventually defeated by a better-resourced

---

[24] Ibid., 62.

[25] Ibid., 17.

[26] Clancy and Crossett, "Measuring Effectiveness in Irregular War", 95.

[27] Christopher Paul, Colin P. Clarke, and Beth Grill, *Victory Has a Thousand Fathers: Sources of Success in Counterinsurgency*, (Santa Monica, California: RAND Corporation, 2010), xxii.; Mao Zedong, *The Red Book of Guerrilla Warfare*, trans. Chen Song, ed. Shawn Conners, (El Paso, TX: Norte Press, 2008) Kindle electronic edition, 3.; James Clancy and Chuck Crossett, "Measuring Effectiveness in Irregular War" *Parameters*, Summer, 2007, 93.

insurgent.[28] If the population lives in fear or passively supports the insurgency, then the insurgent can maintain anonymity and conduct operations among the people. From 1988–1998, the Government of Papua New Guinea fought against a secessionist movement on the island of Bougainville. The Government was able to seal off the island and the insurgents from outside interference. However, they never achieved the support of the population, and eventually were forced to grant powers of self-governance to Bougainville.[29] Every insurgency is unique in how much it must rely on the terrain, geography or the population in order to keep its anonymity advantage. Every counterinsurgency, however, must target this anonymity either directly, indirectly or both.[30]

Direct targeting of the insurgent advantage involves focusing government effort on identifying and eliminating the insurgent. Indirect targeting involves eliminating the ability for the enablers to maintain the insurgent's advantage. The proper mix is dependent on the environment and context of the insurgency, but the counterinsurgent must seek to eliminate this advantage if he is to be successful in destroying the insurgency and he must be able to determine if his direct, indirect or mixed approach is working.

METHOD

Since there are multiple approaches to counterinsurgency, what do practitioners and their supporting theorists say constitutes appropriate metrics? The answers to this question will provide

---

[28] Paul, Clarke, and Grill, *Victory Has a Thousand Fathers: Sources of Success in Counterinsurgency*, 19-20.

[29] Ibid., 17-18.

[30] John A. Nagl, Counterinsurgency Lessons from Malaya and Vietnam: *Learning to Eat Soup with a Knife* (Westport, CT: Praeger Publishers, 2002), Kindle electronic edition, location 471.

an initial list of possible metrics relating to regaining advantage and determine if disruption of tangible resources is an existing accepted metric. Are there other ideas on COIN metrics that do not relate exclusively to a singular COIN approach? Do these supposedly universal metrics include or invalidate resource disruption as an appropriate metric? Are there obvious shortfalls to the metrics that the practitioners, theorist and other contributors propose? Finally, does COIN in practice verify that any of these metrics are able to convey who is in the best position to achieve the desire condition?

FINDINGS

The Direct Approach

The direct approach is the most similar to conventional war and the easiest to demonstrate progress toward victory. The direct approach works best when the insurgent is not a representative of the population, and therefore is easy to identify. It is also effective when an insurgency has not yet reach critical mass; that is it has not demonstrated the ability to sustain itself after the initial confrontation with the state.[31] In Malaya, the insurgency primarily consisted of Chinese.[32] The ethic difference between the Malayans and the insurgents decreased the insurgents' ability to remain anonymous. While not all Chinese were insurgents, the counterinsurgents did at least have a way to distinguish the friendly population from possible enemies. This approach is also more useful when the cause of the insurgency has limited relevance to the plight of the population.[33] The urban focused approach that Chinese communists

[31] Clancy and Chuck Crossett, "Measuring Effectiveness in Irregular War", 92.

[32] Ibid., 93.

[33] Mao Zedong, *The Red Book of Guerrilla Warfare*, trans. Chen Song, ed. Shawn Conners (El Paso, TX: Norte Press, 2008) Kindle electronic edition, 4.

used from 1927 to 1930 was completely ineffective. Mao transformed the cause, and instead grew the insurgency from the rural population with great success.[34] The focoists in Central America sought to incite a revolution through military action prior to gaining the support of the population.[35] The lack of an enabler denied the ability of the insurgent to operate anonymously, allowing the conventional force to maintain asymmetry.[36] In all of these environments, the lack of military uniforms and insignia did not preserve the insurgent anonymity. In environments in which there is a clear delineation between the insurgent and the people, and no place for the insurgent to run and hide, the COIN force can employ the direct approach to great effect.

The direct approach, understanding that the insurgent force represents a discrete set of the population, can often times consist of tactics similar to those used in conventional war. Since insurgent anonymity is weak, the advantage lays with the counterinsurgent force. If, however, the insurgent does have strong anonymity, the direct approach must rely on other, often repressive measures to destroy insurgent anonymity. Roger Trinquier, a French military commander who fought against Algerian insurgents captured what he considered lessons learned in his book in *Modern Warfare: A French View of Counterinsurgency*. He provides a comprehensive approach to directly targeting insurgents who enjoyed strong anonymity. He first discussed the need to have a robust intelligence network with the responsibility of identifying political subversives and insurgent forces. He then describes the process of generating security forces at the local level,

---

[34] Nagl, *Counterinsurgency Lessons from Malaya and Vietnam: Learning to Eat Soup with a Knife,* Kindle location 377.

[35] Frank Zimmerman, "Why Insurgents Fail: Examining Post-World War II Failed Insurgencies Utilizing the Prerequisites of Successful Insurgencies as a Framework" (thesis, Naval Postgraduate School, March 2007), Kindle electronic edition, location 407.

[36] Gordon A Craig and Felix Gilbert, *Makers of Modern Strategy: from Machiavelli to the Nuclear Age*, ed. Peter Paret (Princeton: Princeton University Press, 1986) Kindle electronic edition, 850.

turning the area of operations into a police state. The conventional military force, according to Trinquier, should then hunt down and collect the insurgents for the purpose of both eliminating the insurgent network and in order to take prisoners that can identify remaining elements of the insurgency.[37]

If the direct approach tactics are successful, then the insurgent force no longer exists or is no longer willing to oppose the clearly superior government forces. Measuring this success becomes relatively easy when compared to more complicated approaches to counterinsurgency. The counterinsurgent will first need to have a firm understanding of the insurgent network. Without exposing the organization, the counterinsurgent can neither employ his tactics nor determine his effectiveness; therefore, a commander will first ask, "Do I know what I am up against?" The fewer blank spaces on the insurgent organization chart the better. The next metric involves the accuracy of this information. The question, "Has my intelligence led to positive identification and elimination of the proposed target?" The body count metric provides the final confirmation that the tactics are working.[38] If the counterinsurgent continues to kill the insurgent, then the insurgency will eventually go away, or so the logic goes.

Measuring the effectiveness of direct targeting goes beyond just counting dead or captured insurgents. The British considered a change in the population's behavior as a reasonable metric when countering the Iraqi uprising in 1920. Protests against underrepresentation had grown so violent that British troops were forced to retreat from their garrisons. In order to regain asymmetric advantage over the insurgency, the British dispatched troops from India. Through

---

[37] Roger Trinquier, *Modern Warfare: A French View of Counterinsurgency*, trans. Daniel Lee (London: Pall Mall Press Ltd., 1964), 45-46.

[38] Field Manual 3-24 *Counterinsurgency* (Washington DC: Government Printing Office, September 2006), 5-27.

heavy-handed tactics, government restructuring and addressing grievances, the British ended the protests.[39]

Not all insurgencies have weak anonymity. Sometimes seeking and destroying the insurgent forces means operating among the population. In these situations, the direct approach can produce the opposite of the desired result. Severely oppressive actions in an effort to identify who is loyal to the government and who is not can generate hostility towards the government and cause the insurgency to grow.[40] Therefore, the metrics listed above can be incredibly deceiving. When the insurgent operates among the population, as the counterinsurgent exposes more of the network, he simultaneously increases the size of the network. As the body count metric demonstrates progress toward eliminating the insurgency, the insurgency grows.

The direct action metrics are somewhat discredited following the US war in Vietnam, but they are logical. Clausewitz wrote:

> Still, no matter what the central feature of the enemy's power may be—the point on which your efforts must converge—the defeat and destruction of his fighting force remains the best way to begin, and in every case will be a very significant feature of the campaign.[41]

Determining if the pro-government force has destroyed the insurgent force and stopped the anti-government behavior is the most certain way to determine who has the advantage. However, if the direct approach is not relevant to the environment because the insurgent enjoys strong anonymity enabled by a connection to the population or by favorable terrain and geography, then the metric is irrelevant. The counterinsurgent must instead adopt an indirect approach, which will have its own, less direct metrics.

---

[39] Clancy and Crossett, "Measuring Effectiveness in Irregular War" , 92.

[40] Ibid., 90-93.

[41] Clausewitz, *On War*, 596.

The Indirect Approaches

Terrain based

As already discussed, an insurgent must prevent the counterinsurgent from using superior weaponry, resourcing, mobility, and armor to his advantage. One way the insurgent can do this is by operating from an area outside the counterinsurgent's influence. This can occur where terrain and geography are favorable to the insurgent. David Galula, also a product of the French counterinsurgency in Algeria, described geography favorable to the insurgent in his book *Counterinsurgency: Theory and Practice*. He wrote:

> To sum up, the ideal situation for the insurgent would be a large landlocked country shaped like a blunt-tipped star, with jungle-covered mountains along the borders and scattered swamps in the plains, in a temperate zone with a large and dispersed rural population and a primitive economy.[42]

Denying the insurgent the ability to rely on favorable terrain must first begin with geographic isolation. The insurgent must not have access to a third party sponsor or terrain that allows for continued sustenance and recruiting. Israeli security forces clamped down on Palestinian terrorist and separatist activity by improving border security and executing effective blockades against third party involvement. From 1989 and into the 1990s, the Israeli government increasingly restricted the flow of traffic and resources into Palestinian territories.[43] A reduction in insurgent initiated attacks followed the increased isolation of the Palestinian insurgents.[44]

Favorable terrain is not exclusive to the macro level. Ingress and egress routes from insurgent held terrain offer the means for the insurgent to commute to the fight and remain

---

[42] Galula, *Counterinsurgency Warfare: Theory and Practice,* Kindle location 471.

[43] Nathan W. Toronto, "Forty Years of COIN: The Israeli Occupation of the Palestinian Territories", Joint Force Quarterly, issue 50 (3rd Quarter), 2008, 83, 89.

[44] Ibid, 79.

anonymous without ever requiring the support of the population. Route interdiction or

reengineering of routes to deny raid style attacks can mitigate the insurgent's ability to operate

without COIN force interference. The British government created a figurative "Ring of Steel" in

Belfast to counter the Irish Republic Army's ability to enter, attack, and retreat without ever

encountering risk. According to Stephen Gibbs:

> The preventative measures included re-patterning traffic, search points, and closed circuit television cameras. All of these types of interventions increased the effort and the risk involved in conducting attacks in those cities.[45]

As with the Palestinian case, the British government was able to reduce violence in the

population center, a sure sign of effective tactics.[46]

The terrain based approach to counterinsurgency however, often times does not attempt

to interdict the insurgent, but instead chases the insurgency in a search and destroy type

operation. Sir Robert Thompson, possibly because he first conducted a counterinsurgency in

terrain favorable to the counterinsurgent, described an almost linear approach to denying the

insurgent sanctuary in terrain. He wrote:

> But the concept as a whole is designed to secure a firm base and then to expand from that into disputed, and finally in enemy controlled, territory. If the program is strategically directed, and supported by the Armed Forces, it becomes an offensive advance which will wrest the military initiative from the insurgent. This is far more aggressive, because it is more effective than launching thousands of operations with hundreds of troops in each, all wading through the paddy fields with the rifles cocked to no purpose.[47]

---

[45] Stephen Gibbs, "Applying the Theory and Techniques of Situational Criminology to Counterinsurgency Operations: Reducing Insurgency Through Situational Prevention" (thesis, Naval Post Graduate School, June 2010), Kindle electronic edition, location 418.

[46] Ibid., Kindle location 106.

[47] Robert Thompson, *Defeating Communists Insurgency: Experiences from Malaya to Vietnam* (London: Chatto and Windus Ltd., 1967), 12.

Unfortunately, this method assumes the counterinsurgent force can go everywhere the insurgent can go without ceding any ground. Often times the opposite is true and the insurgent knows it.[48]

Instead of chasing the insurgent, other terrain-based approaches cede some ground to the insurgent but prevent the insurgent from ever realizing his political aims by maintaining a secure environment in the population centers. The Turks followed this approach by:

> …drastic measures to separate the insurgents from the population in the mountain villages in the area of conflict, aggressively pursued the insurgents into the mountains, sought to cut off cross-border support to them, and, most tellingly, made a political deal with extra national hosts to capture the authoritarian leader of the PKK…[49].

As each case demonstrates, the terrain-based approach denies the insurgent the ability to conduct an attack against government controlled territory. Therefore, a reduction of violence is the primary metric of the terrain-based approach. If COIN forces use this approach to eventually finish off the insurgency, either through massive search and destroy missions or through siege style operations, then a discernible drop in insurgent personnel and resources will indicate effectiveness. A reduction in insurgent resources also confirms the effectiveness of geographic isolation of the insurgency as the Turks demonstrated.

Population Based

There are environments in which the insurgent cannot operate outside of the range of influence of the counterinsurgent force, and therefore must rely on the population as a cloak of invisibility. Even the terrain-based approaches often begin with displacing the insurgency from

---

[48] G. L. Lamborn, *Arms of Little Value: The Challenge of Insurgency and Global Instability in the Twenty First Century* (Havertown, Pennsylvania: Casemate Publishers, 2012), Kindle electronic edition, location 3391.

[49] Paul, Clarke, and Grill, *Victory Has a Thousand Fathers: Sources of Success in Counterinsurgency*, 16.

population centers, as Sir Robert Thomson described above. US COIN doctrine is an example of a population centric approach at attacking the insurgent's anonymity. While a significant part of the effort is dedicated to severing the insurgents' link to the population, it does not abandon the logic of directly targeting the insurgent when possible or denying the insurgent a terrain based sanctuary. This makes US COIN doctrine a very inclusive approach to defeating the insurgency, while also making it clear that the population should be the central focus. The omnipresent chart on page 5-3 and 5-5 of FM 3-24 summarizes the approach.

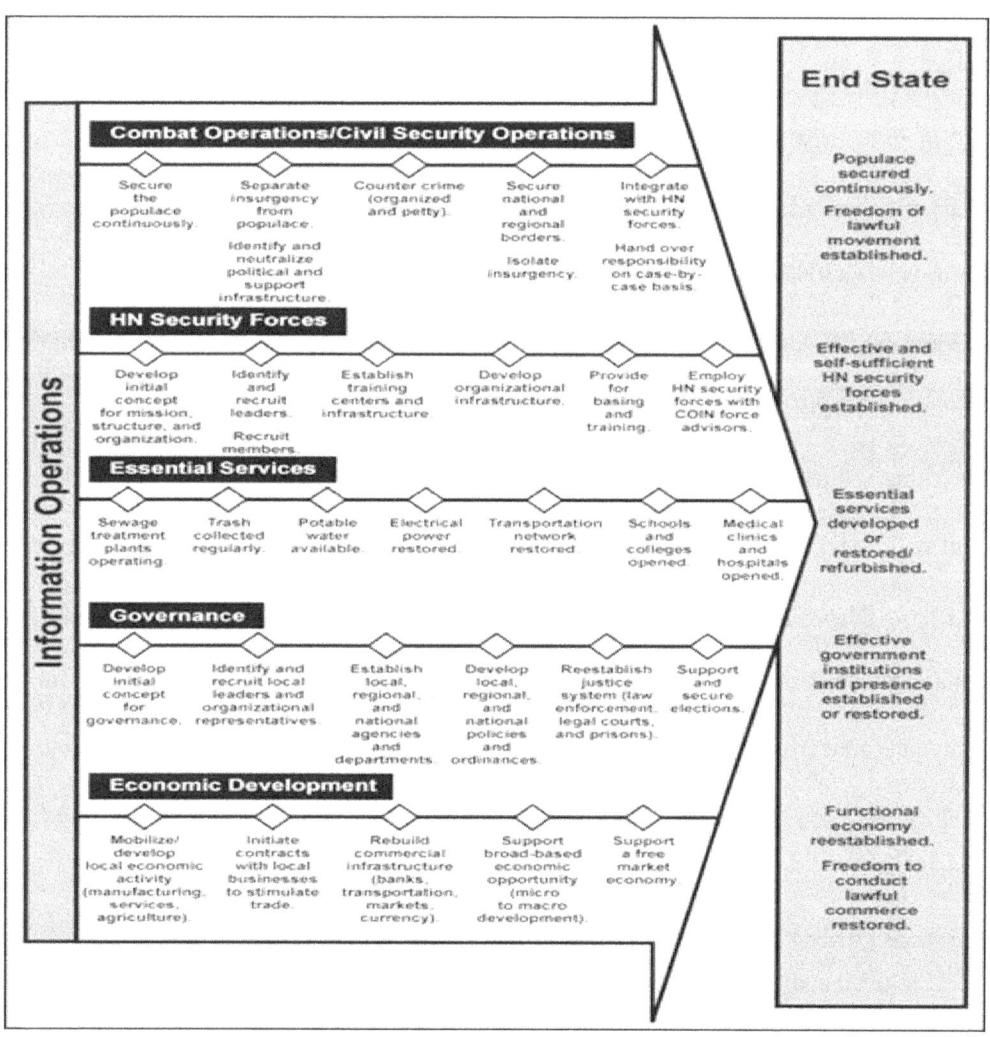

Figure 1: Logical Lines of Operation

Source: Field Manual 3-24 *Counterinsurgency* pg 5-5

The chart depicts five distinguishable logical lines of operation (LLOs) designed to achieve certain conditions in the host nation. When these conditions are satisfied, the expected result is that the insurgent will be defeated or the host nation will no longer require the assistance of the US military in countering the insurgent. The chart depicts a desired endstate (sic) detailing exactly what each LLO should achieve. By executing tactical tasks, monetary investment, training programs, and key engagements, the COIN force should seek to destroy the insurgent network, develop the host nation government, improve the economic condition and infrastructure of the host nation, and improve the capability of the host nation security forces. One should not consider this list exhaustive or prescriptive, but it is the fundamental example for the US Army operating in an insurgent environment.[50] While not a rigid playbook, this manual is the reference for military planners when conducting COIN operations, and therefore, has likely inspired many of the actions of COIN forces.[51]

The first LLO, combat operations, consists of identifying, isolating and eliminating the insurgent and political subversive network. It is the only LLO that focuses a plurality of the tactical actions against the insurgent elements as opposed to the population. This LLO is most congruent with the direct approach favored by Roger Trinquier. There is a major difference between this LLO and the direct approach, however. While the direct approach is solely focused on eliminating insurgents, the combat operations LLO is focuses on eliminating the population's fear of the insurgent while increasing its confidence in the capability of the conventional or pro-government forces. As the COIN force continues to execute successful combat operations, the

[50] Field Manual 3-24 *Counterinsurgency*, 5-7.

[51] Raphael S. Cohen, "A Tale of Two Manuals", *Prism* Vol 2, no. 1, Features, (December 2010) 89-91.

population will grow less and less afraid of the insurgent elements.[52] Eventually, the COIN force will successfully exterminate the insurgents and subversives.

The governance LLO seeks to create a capable, unified organization that can lead and prosecute counterinsurgency on the political level. This body must be able to address root causes of the insurgency, provide a clear vision that offers an alternative to both the present and what the insurgent is offering, and must be able to manage all elements of power, including the military, to isolate, identify, and counter the politically subversive activity. Sir Robert Thompson insists that COIN is actually the government's fight. Of his five principles of counterinsurgency, all begin with the government, not the military, leading or taking action. He adequately argues that a capable, functioning government is a precursor to victory in counterinsurgency.[53] Galula also emphasized the importance and primacy of government in a COIN fight explaining that the current government's existence is ultimately at stake.[54]

The government is likely the only element that has command of the police force, the intelligence services and military. This flexibility, which resides exclusively in the government, can allow it to tailor the proper security and development effort to each area. It is also the government that, in theory, represents the rule of law or predictable, established order.[55] If the government can function based on the efforts of the COIN force, or due to its own existing capability, it should be able to identify problems that are causing the population to turn against it, identify the areas that are of most concern, select the most appropriate force or conglomeration of

---

[52] Trinquier, *Modern Warfare: A French View of Counterinsurgency*, 43.

[53] Thompson, *Defeating Communists Insurgency*, 51.

[54] Galula, *Counterinsurgency Warfare: Theory and Practice*, 41-42.

[55] Thompson, *Defeating Communists Insurgency*, 68.

forces to deal with the area, and take action to bring the population back into support of the government.

The next two LLOs focus on development. Both economic and infrastructure development (labeled in FM 3-24 as essential services) are characterized by the need to win the hearts and minds of the local population. With two opposing forces trying to operate and gain power in the same terrain, many locals are reluctant to choose a side.[56] By targeted development involving construction projects, civil management training that improves the daily lives of the locals, and by creating an environment in which locals can experience economic security or even upward mobility, the government and COIN force, as the entity which delivers these improvements, could become the preferred entity and thus deny any incentives the insurgent has to offer.[57] When a local resident believes in the legitimacy and capability of the host nation government because of its ability to improve the general welfare, there is no need for that local to take up arms against the government or assist those who do. Additionally, this approach seeks to attack the underlying causes of the insurgency so that the population has no reason to seek an alternative to the government. While the combat operations LLO seeks to physically separate the insurgents from the population, these LLOs, enabled by capable governance, seek to psychologically separate the insurgent from the population.

The final line of effort, security, entails protecting the population from the insurgent threat. Galula explained that a population living in fear of the insurgent is not a population that can support the government forces.[58] The counterinsurgent then must focus on separating the

---

[56] Galula, *Counterinsurgency Warfare: Theory and Practice,* Kindle location 808-825.

[57] Thompson, *Defeating Communists Insurgency*, 68.

[58] Galula, *Counterinsurgency Warfare: Theory and Practice,* 37.

population from the insurgent via establishment of a figurative wall of security. This security element should certainly consist of the counterinsurgent forces, but should also include security elements born of the population that are capable of defending against insurgent forces in their own neighborhood. In contrast to the combat operations, this LLO does not attempt to seize the initiative in the fight against insurgents. Instead, this is a defensive approach that shields the population from the efforts of the insurgents, rendering them either irrelevant or forgotten. The entire security apparatus must physically separate the insurgents if necessary and in fact psychologically separate the insurgent from the population. It is the link between the population and the insurgent that allows insurgents to conduct attacks and then fade back in to the population.[59] No amount of economic development or government reform will endear the population to the counterinsurgent cause if the population lives in fear.[60] Once the population feels secure it will not fear sharing intelligence with the counterinsurgent forces, it will enjoy the benefits of the government's efforts to address the causes of the insurgency, and it will no longer have to remain at best neutral in a fight between mutually exclusive agents.

These five LLOs graphically depict a comprehensive approach to denying the population as a potential enabler to insurgent anonymity. The metrics that FM 3-24 offers also relate to the population, but are much more concerned with how the population behaves in the presence of the counterinsurgent. The below table lists example metrics:

---

[59] Long, *On Other War: Lessons from Five Decades of RAND Counterinsurgency Research*, 16.

[60] Galula, *Counterinsurgency Warfare: Theory and Practice*, 37.

Table 1. Selected progress indicators according to FM 3-24

Acts of violence
Human movement and religious attendance
Presence and activity of small and medium-sized businesses
Level of agricultural activity
Presence or absence of associations
Participation in elections
Government services available
Tax revenue
Employment/unemployment rate

Source: Created by Author, based on list in FM 3-24, 2006, page 5-28

This chart demonstrates that the metrics associated with the population centric approach are often indicators of the attitude and comfort level of the populace. Unfortunately these metrics appear to be more appropriately described as Measures of Effort, a phrase coined by COL Gregory Fontenot (U.S. Army, retired) in Bosnia to measure mission accomplishment according to work performed instead of effects of work performed.[61] They seem to measure how well the COIN force has performed along each line of effort, but not how the insurgent force has influenced the insurgent's ability to maintain anonymity or retain symmetry in the fight. US forces operated under the same misguided thought process in Vietnam, measuring the impact of their actions on population support instead of measuring the impact of their actions on the enemy.[62]

---

[61] Russell W. Glenn and S. Jamie Gayton, *Intelligence Operations and Metrics in Iraq and Afghanistan* (Santa Monica, California: RAND Corporation, 2008), 42.

[62] David Strachan-Morris, "Swords and Ploughshares: An Analysis of the Origins and Implementation of the United States Marine Corps' Counterinsurgency Strategy in Vietnam Between March 1965 and November 1968" (doctoral thesis, University of Wolverhampton, December 2010), 17-20.

RAND

Opinions on metrics are not exclusive to doctrine or COIN theorists. Since the 1950s, RAND has conducted extensive research on counterinsurgency, including how to prosecute it and how to measure it.[63] In *Embracing the Fog*, RAND researcher Ben Connable argues for a narrative, decentralized metric to determine if the COIN force is separating the population from the insurgent.[64] Sympathy for this approach is born of a few different paradigms. First is the idea that the commander on the ground always knows best the reality of his or her assigned area.[65] Second is that a COIN environment is so complex, formalized metrics do not measure contextually relevant data. Because only those closest to the situation can know the complexity and context of the immediate environment, then a higher echelon command would never be capable of constructing an appropriate metric.

While his argument is successful at pointing out the failure of past COIN forces to develop relevant metrics, it does not automatically follow that the local commander would be able to do it. Commanders do not inherently have knowledge of COIN effectiveness simply because they are close to the ground.[66] In the current force, there is no concerted effort to train current or future commanders on how to develop metrics.[67] Military Advisory Command

---

[63] Long, *On Other War: Lessons from Five Decades of RAND Counterinsurgency Research*, 2.

[64] Ben Connable, *Embracing the Fog of War: Assessments and Metrics in Counterinsurgency* (Santa Monica, California: RAND Corporation, 2012), 219.

[65] Sun Tzu, *The Art of War*, trans. Samuel Griffith (Oxford: Oxford University Press, 1963), Kindle electronic edition: page 83.

[66] Jonathan Schroden, "Why Operations Fail: It's Not Just the Metrics," *Naval War College Review* 64, no. 4 (Autumn 2011): 99.

[67] Glenn and Gayton, *Intelligence Operations and Metrics in Iraq and Afghanistan*, 53-54.

Vietnam (MACV) experienced a revealing scenario in Vietnam, in which assessments of local areas showed progress while intelligence showed the Vietcong and NVA gaining in numbers and strength.[68] It is inappropriate for a commander to assume that he or she knows the entire fight is progressing toward victory simply because of his or her unit's action. Additionally, relying on a subjective metric does nothing to solve the problem of how to train staffs to develop metrics before arriving to the combat zone.

If the major approaches to counterinsurgency relate to denying anonymity either through identification of the insurgent fighters or through eliminating enablers, then any universal metric must relate to that which anonymity provides. As Geoff Demarest, in his book *Winning Insurgent War*, explains, insurgents use their anonymity to plan, resource, move, stage and attack.[69]

Do the metrics offered by the COIN practitioners, theorist, and contributors address the insurgent's ability to use anonymity to their advantage?

The current list of metrics derived from the above discussion is as follows:

Table 2. Theorist and practitioner metrics

	Direct	Terrain-Based	Population Centric
Body Count	●	●	●
Precision Intelligence	●	●	●
Violence Reduction	●	●	●
Popular Attitude			●
Population Behavior	●		●
Resource Reduction	●	●	
Subjective Assessment			●

Source: Created by Author

---

[68] Graham A. Cosmas, *MACV : The Joint Command in the Years of Escalation, 1962-1967, United States Army in Vietnam* (Washington, DC: United States Army Center of Military History, 2006) 207.

[69] Demarest, *Winning Insurgent War: Back to the Basics*, 20-26.

THE PROBLEM WITH SOME PROPOSED METRICS

Body Count

The body count metric does have logical roots. There is a need to reduce the size and strength of the insurgency. If the COIN force is killing insurgents, it should be ultimate verification that the insurgent no longer enjoys anonymity. The body count metric also is a way to verify the validity of population provided intelligence. If the COIN force kills an insurgent while that insurgent is moving to or from the engagement, or during the execution of an attack, then the population and terrain have not enabled his anonymity. The counterinsurgent has been successful at employing the tools that provide his advantage against the insurgent.

Insurgent death can also occur due to starvation, insurgent infighting, or insurgent caused accident. This type of body count could absolutely be a measure of effectively cutting off the insurgent from their ability to generate resources from the population or geography. A dead insurgent is an under resourced insurgent. This is why the body count metric appears to tie directly to verification that the insurgent no longer enjoys anonymity and is common across all approaches. However, the metric can only be taken in conjunction with other metrics.

The body count metric can be deceiving. As dead insurgents accumulate, the measures employed to kill the insurgents may create more. However, this is not the only reason to question the body count metric. A counterinsurgent might kill more insurgents when the insurgency has more bodies to spare. Insurgents must think in terms of risk.[70] As an insurgency increases its resources and recruits, it becomes less risky to engage the COIN force directly. While the tactical risk may not decrease greatly, the operational risk of losing 100 fighters might be less concerning

---

[70] Gibbs, "Applying the Theory and Techniques of Situational Criminology to Counterinsurgency Operations: Reducing Insurgency Through Situational Prevention", Kindle location 258.

to a large and growing insurgency than it is to a small and dwindling insurgency. Again, the body count metric indicates the exact opposite of its intended indication. The body count metric, therefore, is useful only if the COIN force can link it to demonstrating a shrinking insurgency.[71] If not, it is useless.

Violence Reduction

A reduction in violence, at face value, is a sensible metric. Its commonality across all approaches strengthens its credibility as a metric. It is also directly related to demonstrating the insurgent's inability to use anonymity as an advantage since it relates to the ability to stage and conduct attacks. The saliency of this metric allowed GEN David Petraeus to frame the success of the surge in Iraq in terms of violence reduction.[72] It unfortunately, also has some shortfalls as a standalone, universal metric.

Joint Publication 5-0 states:

> During selected phases of a campaign, JFCs could reduce the pace of operations, frustrating adversary commanders while buying time to build a decisive force or tend to other priorities in the OA(Operations Area) such as relief to displaced persons. During other phases, JFCs could conduct high-tempo operations designed specifically to overwhelm adversary defensive capabilities. Assuring strategic mobility preserves the JFC's ability to control tempo by allowing freedom of theater access.[73]

The JP appropriately instructs commanders to control the application of violence in his or her area of operations. If the COIN force can do it, the insurgents can do it. The enemy has control over when they choose to attack, especially if they retain anonymity.

---

[71] Long, *On Other War: Lessons from Five Decades of RAND Counterinsurgency Research*, 39.

[72] David H. Patraeus, Report to Congress on the Situation in Iraq, 10-11 September 2007.

[73] Joint Publication 5-0, *The Operations Process*, III-36.

An increase in violence can actually be a positive indicator. When the population freely

shares accurate intelligence with the counterinsurgent, the COIN force now has the ability to

initiate violence, and has every reason to do so.[74] A decrease in violence can also be attributable

to poor intelligence. If the counterinsurgent has no idea where to find the insurgent, and the

insurgent out of practicality avoids contact with the COIN force, the low level of violence is an

indicator of strong insurgent anonymity.[75]

There are situations in which the insurgent forces do not have control over when to

initiate violence. One situation occurs when the insurgents do not have the means to fight. An

insurgent who has no access to weaponry or logistics is unable to conduct an attack. Therefore,

when the COIN force can link violence reduction to a reduction in resources, it is a reasonable

metric.[76] Just like body count, if not, it is of little value.

Popular Attitude

Popular attitude and behavior is the most popular metric during the wars in Iraq and

Afghanistan.[77] It is also the metric that most closely associates with the COIN force desire to

measure the insurgent's willingness to fight. Even the chapter on developing measurements and

assessment in the US Army Counterinsurgency Field Manual begins with the following quote

from Robert Thompson:

---

[74] Thompson, *Defeating Communists Insurgency*, 169.

[75] Ibid., 169.; Glenn and Gayton, *Intelligence Operations and Metrics in Iraq and Afghanistan*, 60.

[76] Clancy and Crossett, "Measuring Effectiveness in Irregular War", 95.

[77] Mark Moyar, *A Question of Command: Counterinsurgency from the Civil War to Iraq* (New Haven, CT:Yale University Press, 2009), 2.

Much can be learnt merely from the faces of the population in villages that are subject to the clear-and-hold operations, if these are visited at regular intervals. Faces which at first are resigned and apathetic, or even sullen, six months or a year later are full of cheerful welcoming smiles. The people know who is winning.[78]

The chapter does not mention that Thompson also said, "figures of weapons gains and losses are, indeed, one of the most reliable guides to the course of the war."[79] Instead, the chapter, as Table 1 reveals, focuses on indicators of popular attitude and perceptions. Much like body count and violence, any measurable way to show that the COIN force has popular support seems like a reasonable metric.

Since the population is one element that can enable insurgent anonymity, a public that supports the COIN force should deny the insurgent anonymity. Geoff Demarest outlines the underlying reasons separating the insurgent from the population can contribute to mission success. In arguing that insurgents, in order to sustain their fight, rely on sanctuary, lines of retreat and the lack of government interference, it is clear that they require at a minimum the passive support of the population.[80] While COIN force efforts alone may not motivate the population to rid the town of subversives and insurgents, it will prevent the ability of the insurgent to intimidate the populace into masking insurgent movement. Anytime that a member of the population feels secure enough to tell an insurgent or subversive "no" is a small victory.

Smiles, however, can be deceiving. They do not necessarily indicate actual support. In fact, in wars of this nature, people may devote extra effort to exhibit behavior contrary to how they actually feel in order to survive. Stathis Kalyvas refers to this "preference falsification" in

---

[78] Field Manual 3-24 *Counterinsurgency*, 5-26.

[79] Thompson, *Defeating Communists Insurgency*, 39.

[80] Demarest, *Winning Insurgent War: Back to the Basics*, 25.

order to prove that the two sides in the fight need to alter the population's behavior, not their attitudes.[81]

Even the RAND Corporation experienced a fracturing divide over the question of attitude, morale, and the ability to measure it. The research institute developed a morale study to better gauge the attitude of the Viet Cong (VC) supporters. Within the same organization and using the same study, Leon Gouré and others believed that the VC was losing support, while Konrad Kellen and other believed the contrary.[82] Measuring support, morale, or will power, even when using statistics and science, resulted in a highly subjective and indecisive outcome. Imagine asking a tactical unit to assess the morale of the enemy in an effort to determine its effectiveness.

Demarest argues that what the insurgents need from the population is not love and admiration, but rather a place to move, rest, operate, plan, and store supplies and equipment.[83] When they can muscle their way to achieving these locations, they can continue to gain strength; when they are unable to do so, the counterinsurgent has the upper hand. The insurgent must also have food, military equipment and supplies, and intelligence. Trinquier says that even aid and economic development can wind up in the hands of the insurgent if it is afforded to a population under insurgent influence.[84] According to RAND researcher Charles Wolfe, Jr., insurgents gather all of these resources from the population or a third party sponsor. The battle for the population then is not to undermine the reasons for the insurgency or to influence the hearts and minds of the

---

[81] Stathis Kalyvas, *The Logic of Violence in Civil War* (New York, NY: Cambridge University Press, 2006), 93, 100.

[82] Long, *On Other War: Lessons from Five Decades of RAND Counterinsurgency Research*, 7-9.

[83] Demarest, *Winning Insurgent War: Back to the Basics*, 20-26.

[84] Trinquier, *Modern Warfare: A French View of Counterinsurgency*, 50.

people. It is to alter the behavior of people. It is to affect the sustainability of the insurgency. One can now view the importance of the population in terms of the tangible resources it provides to the insurgent force instead of how favorable the government appears relative to the insurgent force.[85]

Tangible Resources

There is a reason this metric is being introduced last. A pattern forms across all of the other metrics involving tangible resources. Every metric is appropriate as long as it is connected to a reduction in tangible resources. Body count that actually shrinks the insurgency is a reasonable metric. Violence reduction caused by a lack of resources is a reasonable metric. Popular attitude, as long as it occurs in conjunction with the population refusing resources to the insurgent is a reasonable metric. Could it be that a reduction in tangible resources is the universal metric to determine who enjoys asymmetric advantage in counterinsurgency?

COIN IN PRACTICE

In *Victory Has a Thousand Fathers*, Christopher Paul, Colin Clarke, and Beth Grill analyzed every insurgency from 1978 to 2008 to determine which COIN approaches led to COIN success and which approaches led to insurgent victory. The past thirty years provide an excellent benchmark since conditions relating to mass media, logistics and weaponry are comparable to conditions that exist today. According to the study, the single approach that was associated with every COIN victory for the past thirty years was "denying tangible resource support." In every COIN loss, the COIN force was unable to or did not attempt to deny tangible resource support.[86]

---

[85] Charles Wolfe, Jr, *Insurgency and Counterinsurgency: New Myths and Old Realities* (Santa Monica, California: RAND Corporation, 1965), 5.

[86] Paul, Clarke, and Grill, *Victory Has a Thousand Fathers: Sources of Success in*

The conclusion of this study offered a menu of best practices and stated that successful COIN requires a combination of approaches. RAND actually assessed the progress of the war in Afghanistan using the number of best practices employed as the metric.[87] By identifying a singular approach that is so highly associated with success and so easily translated into numbers or statistics, *Victory Has a Thousand Fathers* actually revealed proper metric for COIN forces.

It is now clear that there exists a direct relationship between what should be done and how it should be measured. COIN theory says to attack insurgent elements directly and indirectly in order to separate the insurgent from his ability to rely on the population or the terrain. COIN practitioners include disrupting tangible resource support as an appropriate metric. Every other proposed metric has shortfalls unless liked with resource reduction. COIN in practice reveals that disrupting insurgent tangible resource support is the most effective way to win in counterinsurgency. Measuring insurgent tangible resource support is a far more concrete metric that measuring popular support, government corruption, or enemy influence. It is also a more concrete way of determining if the COIN force has separated the insurgent from the population. Fortunately, COIN practice has revealed that this metric is not only appropriate but possibly the most relevant. Not only is it relevant and required; it is possible.

MEASURING THE METRIC

It Is Possible

Measuring the amount of tangible resources the enemy has on hand and if that amount is decreasing or increasing might seem like a nice idea, but can one actually measure it? The French

---

Counterinsurgency, 70.

[87] Christopher Paul, *Counterinsurgency Scorecard: Afghanistan in Early 2011 Relative to the Insurgencies of the Past 30 Years* (Santa Monica, California: RAND Corporation, 2011)

in Algeria and the British in Malaya certainly wanted to determine their effect on insurgent tangible resources. They both measured weapons captured. This did not, however, tell them how many the enemy actually had to spare.[88] This metric must look beyond captured weapons or the discovery of weapons caches. It requires a new way of thinking about measuring tangible resources, but it can be done.

In *How to Measure Anything*, Douglas Hubbard says, "Many decision makers avoid even trying to make an observation by thinking of a variety of obstacles to measurements".[89] Units can even become so overburdened with collection of data, that even the collectors resent the metrics.[90] Because of the reluctance and frustration, Hubbard offers four useful measurement assumptions:

1. Your problem is not as unique as you think

2. You have more data than you think

3. You need less data than you think

4. An adequate amount of new data is more accessible than you think

Hubbard is correct in stating that measuring insurgent tangible resources is not a new or unique effort. RAND researchers were able to identify after the fact which COIN operations were able to deny tangible resource support to the insurgent. MACV was able to do the same during the conflict in Vietnam. The highly criticized Hamlet Evaluation System in Vietnam was the most infamous means of determining effectiveness.[91] The high command, however, was also aware of

---

[88] Clancy and Crossett, "Measuring Effectiveness in Irregular War", 97.; Thompson, *Defeating Communists Insurgency: Experiences from Malaya to Vietnam*, 39.

[89] Hubbard, *How to Measure Anything*, 31.

[90] Glenn and Gayton, *Intelligence Operations and Metrics in Iraq and Afghanistan*, 54.

[91] Anders Sweetland, *Item Analysis of the HES* (Santa Monica, California: RAND

the continuous build up of VC and NVA personnel and resources.[92] Even today, ISAF attempts to improve the security, governance, and development of Afghanistan. Despite the efforts, however, researchers and military leaders are aware that the tactical actions have not diminished the insurgents' ability to maintain their tangible resource support bases.[93] This demonstrates that measuring insurgent resources has been done before and continues to occur to this day.

The remaining assumptions are also useful. Units already have assigned tactical actions that occupy time and resources. Adding the additional burden of conducting surveys, polls, atmospherics, and status reports leads to the frustration mentioned earlier and reduces tactical and operational flexibility. Ideally, collecting the proper information that indicates the trend in insurgent resources requires no additional resources or tasks. Keeping units away from data collection and focused on executing assigned tasks helps to prevent data from becoming the task.

How to Do It

Measures of effectiveness, when related to maintaining asymmetric advantage over the enemy should be organized similar to intelligence requirements. According to Field Manual 3-55 *Information Collection*, in a conventional war of maneuver, a commander will require certain information pertaining to the enemy and his own forces in order to make timely and informed decisions.[94] These Priority Intelligence Requirements (PIR) are questions the commander expects

---

Corporation, 1968), 1.

[92] Graham A. Cosmas, *MACV : The Joint Command in the Years of Escalation, 1962-1967, United States Army in Vietnam* (Washington, DC: United States Army Center of Military History, 2006) 207.

[93] Paul, *Counterinsurgency Scorecard: Afghanistan in Early 2011 Relative to the Insurgencies of the Past 30 Years*, 9.

[94] Field Manual 3-55, *Information Collection* (Washington DC: Government Printing Office, April 2012), 1–1-1–2.

to be answered before or during an operation so that he can always be in the best position to maintain advantage over the enemy. For instance, a commander may plan to commit his reserve only once his force identifies the enemy's main effort. Unfortunately, even in conventional, uniformed combat the enemy does not broadcast the location and composition of his main effort. The commander and his staff must, instead, generate a list of indicators. Indicators are positive or negative evidence of the activities, intentions, or location of the enemy. These indicators, when present and analyzed allow the commander and his staff to make an informed assumption as to the location of the main effort.[95] In order to synchronize the effort that answers these questions, staffs develop an intelligence support matrix.

Below is a rudimentary example of portions of an intelligence support matrix:

Table 3.Sample Matrix

PIR	Indicators
PIR1: When and where will the western corps reinforce?	Enemy forces conducting river crossing vic XC 123 456
	Enemy forces exfiltrating from position on Hilltop 123
	Artillery fires massed vic XC 123 876
	Enemy forces in column formation along supply route green
PIR 2:Is the enemy preparing to conduct a counterattack?	Enemy forces moving out of Redville
	Enemy armor spotted vic XC 123 098
	Increased civilian movement toward coast
PIR 3: Is the enemy preparing to use WMD?	Enemy forces in chem./bio protective gear
	Presence of decontamination vehicles in enemy formations

Source: Created by Author

---

[95] Field Manual 3-55, *Information Collection*, 3–1–3–6.

This chart shows how the units closest to the ground report on simple and direct occurrences within the environment without having to make any judgment calls as to what they mean. The unit is able to execute its tactical mission without devoting additional effort to answering the commander's question. The operational commander and staff can also use this method to confirm or deny operational and tactical effectiveness, using tangible resources as the primary indicator of effectiveness. The first column would contain the question, "What impact are we having on the insurgent's tangible resources?" Suggested indicators that would appear in the next column are listed in the next section.

Before tasking subordinate units with reporting on indicators, the staff should at least understand what they are looking for. In any measurement is it beneficial to start with a baseline. This data does not have to be absolutely correct. Measurement is about reducing uncertainty and not about exact knowledge.[96] Generating a baseline can start with a Fermi-style estimation about what the insurgent has on hand, and then the staff can refine the information over time.[97] If this is not satisfactory, and the COIN force has adequate resources to do so, then the COIN commander can follow the advice of Demarest and conduct an inventory of everything and everybody.[98] Since this is unlikely, estimation will suffice. The indicators will then be based off deviations from the baseline. Massive deviations may require a complete reframing of the baseline and environmental understanding. Minor deviation may simply confirm the accuracy of the initial estimation. Eventually, the COIN force needs to see deviations from the baseline in an advantageous direction or it needs to expand or alter the operational approach.

---

[96] Hubbard, *How to Measure Anything*, 23.

[97] Ibid., 12.

[98] Demarest, *Winning Insurgent War: Back to the Basics*, 4.

The indicators

Size and scale of attacks

With what size force does the insurgent attack? An insurgent force with more manpower and firepower to spare is less restrained, and therefore, better resourced than a force that only attacks small elements.[99] If the insurgent is attacking with larger forces, then it indicates his resources are increasing. Obtaining this indicator does not require any additional effort on the part of the fielded force. They simply need to provide their higher headquarter an estimated size of the enemy force involved in the confrontation. Often units report these estimates upon initiation of the attack in the form of a SALT report. The "S" in SALT refers to size of the enemy force (A, L, and T refer to activity, location and time of the attack).

Solicitation for sponsorship

Interaction with third party sponsors is an indicator that can reveal a resource constrained or resource rich insurgency. Solicitation of foreign powers could be an indicator that local tangible support is fading. This is exactly what the COIN commander wants to see. It contributes to confirming that operations among the population are being effective. Since this information pertains to events occurring outside of the actual area of operations, national intelligence assets obtain it. While these national assets must dedicate resources to obtaining this information, it does not require any additional theater assets to collect.

Equipment characteristics

Foreign influence

---

[99] Ibid., 221.

If a third party sponsor does support the insurgency and foreign equipment finds its way to violent encounters between insurgents and the COIN force, then the tables have turned. This confirms that the current approach is not regaining asymmetric advantage. GEN Casey, MNC-I Commander in 2005 recalls:

> Our analysts believed that the vast majority of suicide bombers were not Iraqi and entered into the country by crossing the Syrian border. They were moved to their targets by facilitation networks along the western Euphrates valley and Tal Afar–Mosul corridor. Accordingly, I directed the MNC-I to conduct operations to defeat those networks and restore Iraqi control to the borders before the December elections. This would become the major MNC-I operational focus in the run-up to the elections as it also continued to focus on securing Baghdad, steady-state counterinsurgency operations across Iraq, and developing the Iraqi security forces.[100]

GEN Casey communicates how the current effort initially forced the insurgency to adopt a different approach to resourcing, a confirmation of effectiveness. Then the insurgents called a new play and landed a touchdown, once again regaining symmetry. They had a new way to resource their operations. Casey was wise to realize that abandoning the present efforts in the populated areas would drive the insurgent back to a population-based insurgency, but additional effort was required to eliminate the insurgent's ability to use terrain and geography to his advantage. The introduction of weapons, materials, and equipment from a third party is a significant indication that the current approach must be altered or expanded to address the insurgents' ability to remain invisible or non-targetable to the COIN force while he increases resources and commutes from his source of logistic to the point of attack. This indicator will likely require certain resources dedicated to determining the origin of insurgent equipment, but it does not require the unit closest to the ground to determine origin of enemy equipment. The tactical unit simply captures, collects, or locates the equipment. A specialized exploitation team

---

[100] George W. Casey, Jr., *Strategic Reflections: Operation Iraqi Freedom July 2004-February 2007* (Washington DC: National Defense University Press, 2012), 70.

should determine origin. The origin will indicate if the insurgent has just received a significant injection of sustainability.

Sophistication

Equipment Characteristics also include sophistication of the insurgent resources. Obviously one machine gun is more sophisticated than three rifles and an explosively formed projectile is more sophisticated than C4 taped to a mortar round. Are the attacks the insurgents do execute conducted with weapons that are more sophisticated? Do discovered weapons caches reveal higher or lower sophistication? Tactical units can occasionally answer these questions through standard reporting. On other occasions, specialized experts must provide the answer.

Interaction with population

Another indicator involves how the insurgent interacts with the population. This is the first indicator on the list that will actually involve a tactical unit becoming involved in deliberately collecting data outside of standard reporting. Any report that indicates an enemy more demanding of popular support is an enemy that must sacrifice some anonymity to continue to survive. Kidnappings, robberies, and high taxation are all examples of an insurgent trying to squeeze more resources out of the population. Forced conscription was a method the Vietcong employed in order to generate manpower. A sufficiently resourced insurgent does not need to resort to these measures. Using Kidnapping, robberies and other criminal acts as an indicator can be tricky. The kidnapping of a pro-government leader might indicate something far different from the kidnapping of a financially secure shopkeeper. Much like the violence metric, this indicator is a piece of the puzzle. It also requires the most labor and judgment of any of the indicators listed so far.

This monograph does not provide an exhaustive list of indicators, and every environment will require resource specific indicators. Focusing the indicators on tangible resources, however, is the most appropriate and measurable way for the counterinsurgent determining his impact on the insurgent's link to the advantage enabling mechanisms.

Metrics—Not Tasks

The danger of a tangible metric is the ease with which it can be translated into a task to do. If the commander on the ground realizes that higher headquarters is only interested in the unit's impact on insurgent tangible resources then that commander may tailor tactical actions to seek and destroy insurgent resources rather than address the reason the insurgent has those resources. If a unit spends its time stopping people at the border or hunting down weapons caches, it may miss the larger reason for the insurgency. Commanders in Vietnam felt the pressure to pile up communist bodies because of the emphasis on a body count metric. With a "days in the field" metric, they felt compelled to spend more time on patrol rather than working with the population.[101] These types of activities miss the point. Tangible resource reduction cannot be the focus of action; it has to be the result of action. The benefit of mirroring the intelligence requirement process is that it does not require those closest to the ground to have a role in assessment. The units closest to the ground simply carry on with their assigned tasks and report what they see.

CONCLUSION

The US military cannot ignore the possibility of fighting an insurgency in the future. Unfortunately, there is no way to predict with absolute accuracy where this will be. If there are universal metrics to use in the training and operating environment, then the military should be aware of them. This will help drive the way government leaders resource the military and how

---

[101] Glenn and Gayton, *Intelligence Operations and Metrics in Iraq and Afghanistan*, 50.

units employ those resources in the field. There is no shortage of opinions on what constitutes an appropriate metric for counterinsurgency, so it is critical to make sure that these proposed metrics make sense.

Clausewitz said that in war, one must render the enemy unwilling or unable to fight. COIN theory, doctrine, and practice have not deviated from this timeless wisdom. Despite the adherence to the Clauswitzian logic, conventional wisdom still says that measuring effectiveness in COIN is more difficult than in state on state conflict.[102] It is likely that tying metrics to a preconceived notion about what a victorious war looks like has introduced the confusion. Insurgencies do not normally end with white flags or treaty signing ceremonies. Instead, they typically end in a whimper, without anyone really knowing if the fight has concluded. There have been some instances where the fight appeared to be over only to be resumed once the insurgent felt conditions were right. If metrics instead are tied to maintaining advantage over the insurgent, then the state can stay in a position to achieve its political will. Sometimes this will take altering the way the COIN force is accustomed to fighting. Sometimes it will appropriately require addressing the grievances that started the insurgency. Nevertheless, no matter the method, the COIN force should prevent the insurgent from being able to wage his war without risk. He must be exposed. He must have nowhere to run and hide. He must have no capacity to wage war.

Denying the insurgent the ability to remain invisible to the counterinsurgent requires securing the terrain and having the active support of the population. While the methods to accomplish this are environmentally dependant, an insurgent without these enablers will look the same no matter the environment. He will be starved, low on ammunition, immobile, desperate,

---

[102] Long, *On Other War: Lessons from Five Decades of RAND Counterinsurgency Research*, 39.

and routinely defeated in battle. He will remain so under-resourced that he will eventually be dead.

So many of the theories that inform doctrine appear to focus on attacking the insurgent's willingness to fight by addressing greivences or creating a penopticon. Unfortunately, many COIN metrics involve measuring this aspect, and this becomes not only difficult for the units closest to the ground, but a frustratingly futile endeavor.[103] Measuring the insurgents' willingness, while partially possible through capture of prisoners and defection still does not necessarily reveal an aggregate metric that can indicate if overall the COIN force is winning.[104] Since many of the most devoted insurgents have absolute enmity to the COIN force, then overcoming their will to fight becomes unlikely.[105] Overcoming their means to fight becomes the logical approach and is consistent with the wisdom of Clausewitz.[106] The COIN forces who have done this have won.

Measuring the trend in insurgent tangible resources is possible and likely less costly in terms of resources than conducting polls, survey, and atmospherics that only focus on the effects of COIN priorities. The COIN force should conduct the measurements in a way that requires as little subjective assessment as possible, similar to the way PIRs are answered. With indicators based on the environment that are only analyzed at the operational level, tactical elements can be free to operate and report without being asked to judge or win.

---

[103] Glenn and Gayton, *Intelligence Operations and Metrics in Iraq and Afghanistan*, 55.

[104] Kalyvas, *The Logic of Violence in Civil War*, 106.

[105] Carl Schmitt, *Theory of the Partisan* (New York: Telos Press Publishing, 2007).

[106] Clausewitz, *On War*, 90.

It is absolutely critical that reducing insurgent tangible support does not become the task of the counterinsurgent, but rather the outcome of counterinsurgent effort.[107] Every COIN environment is different. This difference does not simply include the enablers of the insurgency, but also includes the political will and desired political condition of the government and pro-government citizenry and armed forces. A too narrow focus on resource denial as a task could cause a COIN force to make all the wrong moves, just as measuring popular attitudes in a terrain-based insurgency could yield lead to a tremendous amount of futile effort.

There may be other universal metrics that this monograph has not discovered. With a recent insurgency in Libya being supported through Twitter and resourced through thousands of westerners who had absolutely no skin in the fight, insurgencies may move into an entirely new dimension.[108] Countering resources may become so difficult that governments return to the direct and oppressive style of counterinsurgency. Without knowing exactly what the future holds, it is reasonable to at least embrace the metrics that have been functional in the past and the principles that have remained a part of war for all time. People need stuff. Even though the insurgent can change a government without ever driving a tank, he still needs more than an idea. If the shadows afford him the opportunity to obtain and employ the means by which he wages war, then the shadows need to go away. Even when the shadow is illuminated, the government may still not see the man behind the war, but they will see the impact of the figurative illumination. The insurgent will have no more and eventually be no more.

---

[107] Charles Wolfe, Jr, *Insurgency and Counterinsurgency: New Myths and Old Realities* (Santa Monica, California: RAND Corporation, 1965), 20.

[108] Carvin, Andy, "Hacking the New York Times, Tweeting Revolutions, and More", On The Media. National Public Radio, MP3 Audio file. http://www.onthemedia.org/2013/feb/01/, (accessed on February 1, 2013).

BIBLIOGRAPHY

Army Doctrinal Reference Publication 5-0. *The Operations Process*. Washington DC: Government Printing Office, September 2011.

Beckerman, Linda "The Non-Linear Dynamics of War". *Science Applications International Corporation ASSET Group*. 1999. http://www.calresco.org/beckermn/nonlindy.htm, (accessed on March 11, 2013).

Boot, Max. *Invisible Armies: An Epic History of Guerrilla Warfare from Ancient Times to the Present*. New York: Liveright Publishing Corporation. 2013. Kindle electronic edition.

Carvin, Andy. "Hacking the New York Times, Tweeting Revolutions, and More". *On The Media*. National Public Radio. MP3 Audio file. http://www.onthemedia.org/2013/feb/01/.

Casey, George W. Jr. *Strategic Reflections: Operation Iraqi Freedom July 2004-February 2007*. Washington DC: National Defense University Press. 2012.

Center for Military History Publication 70-83-1. *The United States Army in Afghanistan: Operation Enduring Freedom October 2001-March 2002*.

Clancy, James and Chuck Crossett. "Measuring Effectiveness in Irregular War". *Parameters*, Summer, 2007.

Clausewitz, Carl Von. *On War*, trans. And ed. Michael Howard and Peter Paret. Princeton University Press, 1984. Kindle edition.

Cohen, Richard. "A Tale of Two Manuals". *Prism* Vol 2, no. 1, Features. (December) 2010.

Connable,Ben. *Embracing the Fog of War: Assessments and Metrics in Counterinsurgency*. Santa Monica, California: RAND Corporation, 2012.

Cosmas, Graham A. *MACV : The Joint Command in the Years of Escalation, 1962-1967, United States Army in Vietnam*. Washington, DC: United States Army Center of Military History, 2006.

Craig, Gordon A. and Felix Gilbert. *Makers of Modern Strategy: from Machiavelli to the Nuclear Age*. Edited by Peter Paret. Princeton: Princeton University Press, 1986. Kindle electronic edition.

Demarest, Geoff. *Winning Insurgent War: Back to the Basics*. Ft. Leavnworth, Kansas: Foreign Military Studies Office, 2001.

Field Manual 3-24. *Counterinsurgency*. Washington DC: Government Printing Office, September 2006.

Field Manual 3-55. *Information Collection*. Washington DC: Government Printing Office, April 2012.

Galula, David. *Counterinsurgency Warfare: Theory and Practice*. N.P. Fredrick A Praeger, 1966.

Gibbs, Stephen. "Applying the Theory and Techniques of Situational Criminology to Counterinsurgency Operations: Reducing Insurgency Through Situational Prevention" Thesis, Naval Post Graduate School, June 2010. Kindle electronic edition.

Glenn, Russell W. and S. Jamie Gayton. *Intelligence Operations and Metrics in Iraq and Afghanistan*. Santa Monica, California: RAND Corporation, 2008.

Hubbard, Douglass. *How to Measure Anything: Finding the Value of "Intangibles" in Business*. Hoboken, New Jersey: John Wiley & Sons, Inc, 2010.

Joint Publication 5-0. *Joint Operation Planning*. Washington DC: Government Printing Office, September 2011.

Lamborn, G.L. *Arms of Little Value: The Challenge of Insurgency and Global Instability in the Twenty First Century*. Havertown, Pennsylvania: Casemate Publishers, 2012. Kindle electronic edition.

Long, Austin. *On Other War: Lessons from Five Decades of RAND Counterinsurgency Research*. Santa Monica, California: RAND Corporation, 2006.

Mao Zedong. *The Red Book of Guerrilla Warfare*. Translated by Chen Song and edited by Shawn Conners. El Paso, TX: Norte Press, 2008. Kindle electronic edition.

Moyar, Mark. *A Question of Command: Counterinsurgency from the Civil War to Iraq*. New Haven, CT:Yale University Press. 2009.

Nagl, John A. *Counterinsurgency Lessons from Malaya and Vietnam: Learning to Eat Soup with a Knife*. Westport, CT: Praeger Publishers, 2002. Kindle electronic edition.

Patraeus, David H. Report to Congress on the Situation in Iraq. 10-11 September 2007.

Paul, Christopher, Colin P. Clarke, and Beth Grill. *Victory Has a Thousand Fathers: Sources of Success in Counterinsurgency*. Santa Monica, California: RAND Corporation, 2010.

Paul, Christopher. *Counterinsurgency Scorecard: Afghanistan in Early 2011 Relative to the Insurgencies of the Past 30 Years*. Santa Monica, California: RAND Corporation, 2011.

Schmitt, Carl. *Theory of the Partisan*. New York: Telos Press Publishing, 2007.

Schroden, Jonathan. "Why Operations Fail: It's Not Just the Metrics," *Naval War College Review* 64, no. 4 (Autumn 2011).

Strachan-Morris, David. "Swords and Ploughshares: An Analysis of the Origins and Implementation of the United States Marine Corps' Counterinsurgency Strategy in Vietnam Between March 1965 and November 1968", doctoral thesis, University of Wolverhampton, 2010.

Sun Tzu, *The Art of War*. Translated by Samuel Griffith. Oxford: Oxford University Press, 1963. Kindle electronic edition.

Thompson, Robert. *Defeating Communist Insurgency: Experiences from Malaya to Vietnam*. London: Chatto and Windus Ltd., 1967.

Trinquier, Roger. *Modern Warfare: A French View of Counterinsurgency*, trans. Daniel Lee. London: Pall Mall Press Ltd., 1964.

Toronto, Nathan W. "Forty Years of COIN: The Israeli Occupation of the Palestinian Territories". *Joint Force Quarterly*, issue 50 (3rd Quarter). 2008.

Wolfe, Charles Jr. *Insurgency and Counterinsurgency: New Myths and Old Realities*. Santa Monica, California: RAND Corporation, 1965.

Zimmerman, Frank. "Why Insurgents Fail: Examining Post-World War II Failed Insurgencies Utilizing the Prerequisites of Successful Insurgencies as a Framework". Thesis, Naval Postgraduate School, March 2007.